A DAY IN THE LIFE OF A
Beekeeper

by Penny Michels and Judith Tropea
Photography by John Halpern

Troll Associates

Library of Congress Cataloging-in-Publication Data

Michels, Penny.
  A day in the life of a beekeeper / by Penny Michels and Judith
Tropea; photography by John Halpern.
      p.   cm.
  Summary: Describes the daily work of a beekeeper who teaches
biology and keeps his hives as a sideline.
  ISBN 0-8167-2206-4 (lib. bdg.)   ISBN 0-8167-2207-2 (pbk.)
  1. Bee culture—Juvenile literature.   2. Beekeepers—Biography—
Juvenile literature.   [1. Beekeepers.   2. Bee culture.
3. Occupations.   4. Avitabile, Alphonse.]   I. Tropea, Judith.
II. Halpern, John, 1957-   ill.   III. Title.
SF523.5.M53   1991
638.1—dc20   90-11078

The author and publisher would like to thank Alphonse Avitabile, Norman E.
Farmer, and Toby Kiers for their generous assistance and cooperation.

Photo credits: pp. 7, 20, 27, 28 (bottom)—Alphonse Avitabile.

Al Avitabile has been keeping honeybees for years. He is also a biology teacher at the University of Connecticut. Some beekeepers maintain enough hives to earn their living from keeping bees, but beekeeping is Al's favorite hobby. Al loves to share his knowledge of beekeeping with other people. This morning he is awaiting the arrival of a student who wants to find out about bees and bee behavior.

Toby arrives at nine. She is working on a bee project in school, and she has asked Al to help her gain some firsthand information about beekeeping. Toby is excited about the day ahead, but she is also a little scared to work with bees. Al explains that she will not be afraid of bees once she learns about them.

On the way to the hives, Al stops to show Toby
some honeybees working a sumac flower. Bees ob-
tain nectar and pollen from flowers. Nectar is
changed by bees into honey. Sumac is one of the
many flowering shrubs that bees visit. Many sumac
flowers grow on Al's land. This makes it a good
place for bees to live.

When the bees return to the hive, they deposit nectar in one of the cells in a honeycomb. Beekeepers remove the combs as they become filled with honey, and replace them with wax sheets that bees will make into new honeycombs. Al and Toby examine a wax sheet before they get to the hives. The hives are in a spot that is breezy and sunny throughout the year.

Al explains that in winter the hives must be specially wrapped to protect the bees. Wrapping insulates the hives. During the winter, bees survive on the honey and pollen they have stored in their honeycombs. Bees in the wild usually build their nests in cavities, but sometimes the nest of honeycombs is more exposed. The exposed nests are not as likely to survive through the winter.

To prevent themselves from being stung, beekeepers wear protective clothing. Al wears a simple hat with a veil, but since Toby is a beginner she wears a full jumpsuit with a hood. When they get to the hives, she will put gloves on so her whole body will be covered. As Toby suits up, Al reminds her that slow, gentle movements will not alarm the bees, but rapid movements often will.

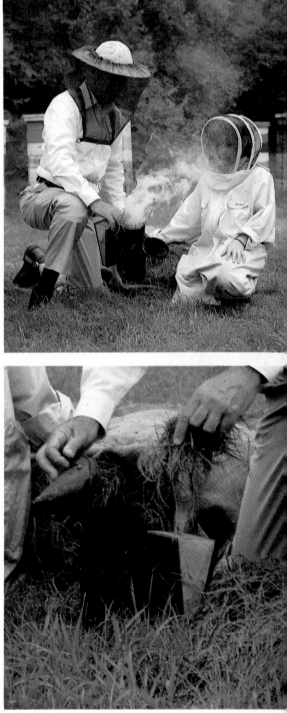

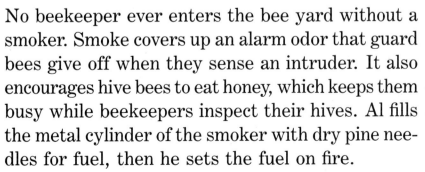

No beekeeper ever enters the bee yard without a smoker. Smoke covers up an alarm odor that guard bees give off when they sense an intruder. It also encourages hive bees to eat honey, which keeps them busy while beekeepers inspect their hives. Al fills the metal cylinder of the smoker with dry pine needles for fuel, then he sets the fuel on fire.

Al spreads the smoke all around the hive to make sure each possible entrance receives smoke. He compares smokers to lion tamers' whips: "The tamer doesn't go into his cage without a whip, and the beekeeper should never open a hive without a smoker." Lions cannot be trained as pets, and neither can bees.

Each box on the hive is called a *super*. Bees glue the hive together with *propolis*, a sticky substance from plants. Al uses his hive tool to take off the hive cover and separate the supers. Beekeepers put shallow supers on top, because they are easier to lift. The deeper ones below serve as brood chambers where eggs develop into bees. Each super can hold up to ten honeycombs.

After smoking the hive again, Al lifts the top super off to give Toby a better view of the inside of a hive. Toby watches closely as Al removes a comb with his bare hands. Al is so comfortable around his bees, he no longer wears bulky gloves. He cautions Toby, however, that beginners should always wear gloves.

After bees deposit nectar in the cells of the honey-comb, they fan their wings to evaporate water from the nectar. When the nectar changes into honey, bees cover, or *cap*, the cells with a thin film of wax. Al shows Toby the wax on the honeycomb. It takes about 20,000 bees to bring in one pound of nectar, and it takes one pound of nectar to make a quarter of a pound of honey.

Although there are many honeycombs in a hive, not all of them are filled with honey at the same time. After inspecting a few different supers, Al and Toby find a super that holds many full honeycombs. Toby selects a honeycomb filled with honey, and now they are ready to take it to the honey house for harvesting.

Al and Toby remove their veils to work in the honey house. The honey house is set up with different machines to extract the honey from the honeycombs. The machines can be dangerous if they are not used properly, so Al must supervise Toby very carefully. The first machine they use is the uncapping knife. Al likes to call it the jiggle knife because it jiggles while it works.

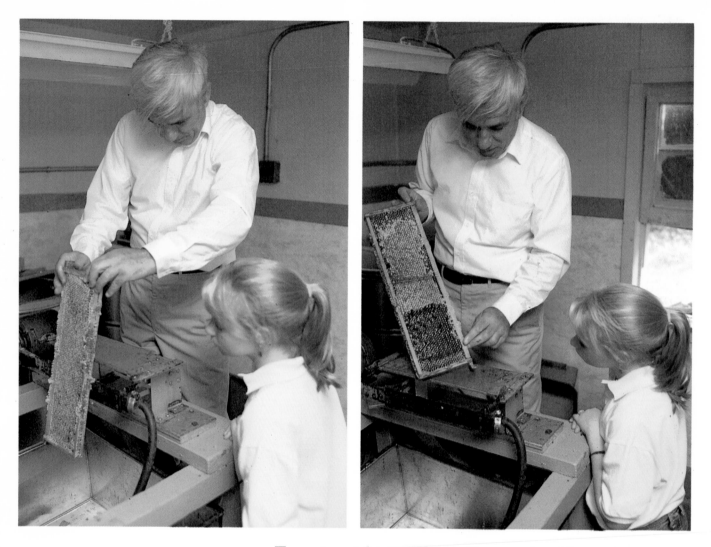

To extract honey from the comb, Al must remove the thin film of wax covering the honey. He holds the comb gently against the jiggle knife. Some bee-keepers uncap their combs by hand, but Al uses the machine because he has so many honeycombs to uncap. As the wax cappings fall into the pan underneath the knife, Al shows Toby the dark, rich honey contained in each cell of the honeycomb.

As much honey as possible should be removed from the comb. Al takes Toby to the extracting machine. The large, stainless steel vat spins very quickly to pull the honey from the comb. Toby loads the comb into the extractor and turns it on.

Al invites Toby to dip her hand into the cappings to taste the fresh honey. Al explains that honey tastes best right after it is extracted from the comb because it is in its purest form. The fresh honey is a welcome treat after a hard morning's work in the bee yard.

After the honey is extracted it must be jarred and labeled. The taste of honey varies depending on what type of flower the bees obtained the nectar from. Al tells Toby to make sure she shuts the door when she leaves the honey house because once a bee "scout" finds the extracted honey, it will alert other bees and they will follow the scout into the honey house to collect the honey.

Honeybee colonies can grow as overcrowded as big cities. When hives become overcrowded, the colony divides itself and about half the bees leave as a swarm. These swarming bees will fly to a nearby object and form a swarm cluster. Al has been asked to remove swarms from many locations. He brings them home and puts them into a new hive. In this way he starts bee colonies.

A more traditional way beekeepers start new hives is by adding "packages" of bees that are sent to them from other beekeepers. Today Al has received a new package of bees. Al is part of a group of beekeepers who breed bees for special traits like gentleness or strong nectar-gathering tendencies. He will add the new bees to an empty hive in order to begin a new colony.

Since there are thousands of bees in each package, it is difficult to get them all to go into the new hive at once. However, once the bees begin to release a scent near the entrance, many bees enter the hive. The bees use their scent glands to attract members of their group toward the hive. Al points out some of the scenting bees on a landing board near the hive's entrance.

Now it is time for Al and Toby to send off a package of his bees, which were bred especially for gentleness, to another beekeeper. The package is a small wooden box with screened sides so the bees can breathe and not be overheated during shipping. To get the bees into the package, they also need a large metal funnel, and of course, the smoker.

A honeycomb consists of many six-sided cells placed next to one another. Strong combs like Al's are created by thousands of bees. When a hive is opened, the bees can be seen covering each of the honeycombs. To make a one-pound package of bees, a beekeeper needs 3,500 bees. Al and Toby will shake almost 10,500 bees from their combs to make a three-pound package.

Al carefully shakes the bees from one of his prize honeycombs into the funnel and down into the package. Toby is worried that they will cling to the comb, but Al shows her that three or four taps of the frame against the funnel dislodge the bees from the comb. The dislodged bees fall through the funnel and into the package.

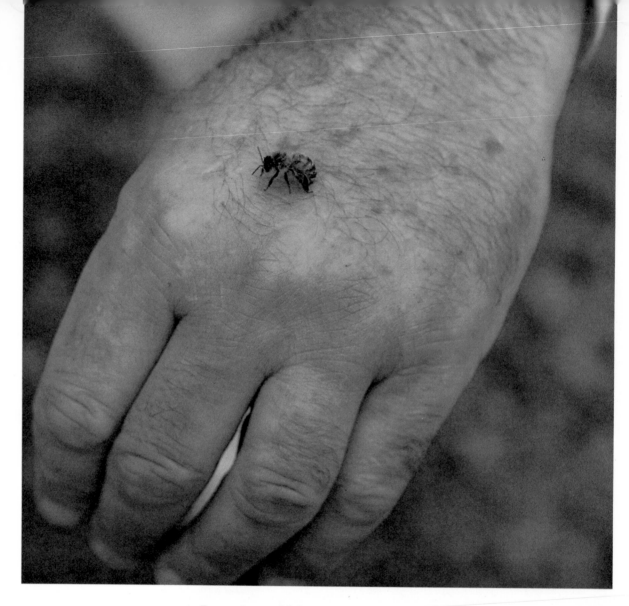

In spite of his calm, quiet treatment of his bees, Al does get stung occasionally. Once the worker bee pierces Al's skin with its barbed sting, it struggles to free itself. The sting, with its poison sac, is ripped from the bee's body. This means the bee will die soon. Al scrapes the sting off with his fingernail. Once the sting is removed, no more venom can enter Al's body, but he is left with a stinging sensation.

In a beehive, the males are called drones and the females may be either workers or queens. The drone has no sting and is larger than a worker bee. Its only job is to mate with the queen. After a drone mates with a queen, it dies. The female workers carry on most of the activities of the colony. They build combs, gather nectar, pollen, propolis, and water, and guard the hive.

Al must locate a queen to put in his package. There is usually only one queen per hive. Queens are normally the only bees who lay eggs to make more bees. Without a queen, the hive would eventually die. If a queen dies, large amounts of royal jelly are fed to a new female larva. Royal jelly causes the development of a queen bee. Other female larvae receive honey for food and they become workers.

Since the queen is the most important part of a bee package, she gets her own separate cage. Al manages to catch her and put her in the cage. The queen cage is suspended in the bee package. Al places the queen cage in the package very carefully, and he makes sure she is securely locked in her cage.

When Al places bees in a new hive, he usually provides them with sugar-water in a jar. But when bees are shipped, this food must be in an unbreakable container. Al fills a small tin with sugar-water and suspends it inside the package, close to the queen. The container has specially sized holes that allow the bees to draw the sugar-water from the can without spilling it in the cage.

Toby covers the package and prepares it for mailing. The worker bees are in place, and the queen is in her cage and ready to go. Al has provided enough food and water for the journey. They put a rush label on the package to be sure that the bees do not die before they arrive at their destination.

When Toby leaves at the end of the day, she carries a jar of honey that Al has given her to use for her report. On Monday she will tell her class everything she has learned about bees and beekeeping. And all her classmates will share the delicious natural treat called honey.

THANK YOU...

...for buying this book from the series "A Monsters Guide to Life... in a Pandemic" written by Laurie Theurer and Katie Lee Koz.

We at Nonviolent Peaceforce (NP) are so grateful to you for supporting us via this wonderful initiative that Katie and Laurie have brought to life. Fifty percent of the profits from all book sales will be supporting NP projects to decrease violent conflict around the world.

Since 2003, NP has focused on creating sustainable peace through unarmed, non-violent civilian protection, training & coaching in nonviolence, and building community through connection. The organization works in countries impacted by violent conflict around the world, such as South Sudan, Myanmar, Iraq, and the Philippines.

NP's newest programing is in response to the increased violence in cities in the U.S. and is now responding to requests to work on community-based projects deescalating and preventing violence at demonstrations and promoting unarmed, civilian led solutions in several cities around the U.S.

To learn more about how you can get involved, and to make a donation, please visit www.nonviolentpeaceforce.org

Thank you again so much for your contribution to making this world a safer place for everyone. Happy reading!

Tiffany Easthom
Executive Director, Nonviolent Peaceforce

CPSIA information can be obtained
at www.ICGtesting.com
Printed in the USA
LVHW072304110221
679069LV00002B/46